MW01113761

STARTING FROM THIRD AVENUE

A Love Story

By David Kherdian

Cascade Press

Published by Cascade Press
under exclusive license from David Kherdian.

Kherdian, David. Starting from Third Avenue: A Love Story

ISBN 978-1-64872-020-8

Inquiries regarding permissions or bulk printing requests should be sent
to info@cascade.press

Inquires with questions to the author should be sent
to tavitnonny@gmail.com

To Nonny

STARTING FROM THIRD AVENUE

CONTENTS

PROLOGUE

I must have been around twelve years old when it came to me as a vision that the greatest thing in life—my life, that is—was to find the person I was meant to spend my life with. It was a wondrous moment that enshrined itself in me as an immutable truth. This unshareable secret remained within, unquestioned, and when in my late thirties I found my soul mate, I was immediately ready—as was Nonny, who would tell me later that her own feelings at a young age were not dissimilar from mine.

Marriage: The peculiar mixture of two strangers joined in an agreed bond that can only be deciphered over time—it being an explicable mystery, but not easily understood, unless engaged in with love, respect, and a belief about oneself and the other—first in faith, and then with a growing commitment that is strengthened by its reality over time.

Our marriage was gifted with certain advantages from the start, which we instantly welcomed: our parents were old country Armenians, and so we grew up with the same foods and mother language, and then, too, we were both independent freelance artists, at the start of our careers, and in our own way we drew on our ancestral histories that easily found their way in our work. All of these attributes were reinforced when we began doing books together, and from all this and also from within our art, we learned still more about ourselves and each other.

Although we suffer now in our advanced age from never having had children, this was a condition that freed us to be the nomadic wanderers we have been all of our lives, an ativisim, neither of us were fully aware of when we met. And we had loving cats, who were always there as integral members, along with the books we created—our surrogate children.

Finally, the reader will want to know how we met, the circumstances surrounding that fateful moment. First of all, we already knew each other's work. Therefore, when at age thirty-seven I took editorship of *Ararat*, an Armenian-American literary magazine in New York, the first call I made from my publisher's office, was to Nonny Hogrogian, to introduce myself and to ask if she would do a cover drawing for my just completed book of poems, HOMAGE TO ADANA. She was acquainted with my work, and knew instinctively, that because I was a poet, she would not likely get paid—so she turned me down, recommending another artist in the city, and providing her number before hanging up. But before I could dial the number, she phoned back and asked to see the manuscript. To make short a long story, she fell in love with me through my poems, and soon after invited me to lunch, to pick up her drawing for my book.

The stage was set. My first words to her, after handing her my coat and hat, was to ask why she wasn't married, to which she replied—somewhat taken aback—that she *would* be. And then I asked what her sign was. When she replied, Taurus, I exclaimed that it would never work, because my first wife was a Taurus. The part of me that knew what was going on then became silent, while the unconscious part remained alert for what might come next.

And that was how we began.

12

Starting From Third Avenue

NEW YORK

THE FIRST DAY

We had lunch with white
wine and cheese. I brought
that, you made the soup.
Armenian olives and bread.
And the *mezzes* you served
in small Oriental bowls.

When it was done, and after
we had talked, I put on my
hat and then removed it at
the door to give you a
parting hug and a kiss on
the cheek.

First hours, and then days
later I began to realize
that nothing is as casual
as that for which the end
is not yet written

NONNY

While I imagine that I am
about to write this poem,
I also imagine that you
have begun a new drawing
for your book. And as the
form of it begins to come
into existence in my mind,
I realize that it is your
face I am drawing with these
unformed words. With memories,
and images I cannot seize
or hold. We hardly know each
other, we just recently met,
yet I am longing for you as
if we were lovers.

THE IDEA

I like the idea of your being
Nonny Hogrogian.
Walking down the street,
black coat on; orange, rust–
brown jumper. Oh, your shoes.
You stop at a store window
for the reflection given back.
Then turning, stepping,
(held by this secret embrace)
you are walking,
walking through magic
into this turning year.

THE FIRST NIGHT / 1

You say, are you tired, would you
like to sleep? And then scouch down
and fit yourself beneath my enveloping
arm, for you know already the position
we will take for sleep. If I move, I find
you turning as I turn. Whatever
occurs, you are ready in advance: more
love, a kiss—whatever is happening
you make it happen right.

This is our first night together, but
already you know how the marriage
bed lies.

TO NONNY

There is a green light cast from
your hanging window plants that
pours over your shoulder as you work.

You are murmuring and sighing and
I am imagining the drawing that is
moving down through the tributaries of
your body into your arm and down through
your fingertips onto the paper that
is lit by your face.

I want to sit here with my back to
you for just one more moment to
enjoy these thoughts of you before
getting up and writing down the quiet
of what has taken place.

NONNY YOUR SHOES

O your tanned low-heeled shoes,
that wear at the toes your faintly
blushed & rosy cheeks, sit and stare
out at me from beside the chair,
beside your table, that I sit and
write on while you are away—over
into the next room, where you are
making a drawing that will, if
I am lucky, be as lovely
as your feet.

AH, NONNY NONNY

From far away somewhere you bring
your red long-nozzled watering can
from the kitchen and begin pouring
water from yourself to your plants.

Talking to the first one and then
murmuring to each of the rest, you
move around your little apartment
on naked sunny feet.

They know your red long-nozzled
watering can and have adjusted long
ago to this cramped city life, but
what must they think of my masculine
presence in this creatively ordered
until now feminine house.

THE WAIT

I have never before been taken so close
to the idea of death—the fear of failing
health, of accident—or that there might
be some cosmic law that would declare our
love a mistaken intent.

When you left tonight for your class, I had
to lie down, to feel through to myself
from this altered posture, and to look at
my life in this way from within the eyes
of your walls and your plants.

If your plants speak to me, if your walls
talk to me, you must come and tell me
their message, as I also wait on your
feminine patience to calm this man fear

OF HUSBANDS AND WIVES

The shape of my Armenian nose is slowly
becoming the distorted shape of the noses
for the figures you are drawing for your
book of tales from the pen of Grimm. The
mustache on the old flounder catcher from
the tale "The Fisherman and His Wife" is
also mine—and all the women seem to have
your funny nose (seemingly connected to
your eyebrows in a mask) and your upturned
innocent mouth that smiles.

Through my poems through your art we are
re-creating the race in an image that is ours.
The gentleness of my art, the tenderness of
yours, were there long before we met so will
not go away—because it was for a time such
as this that we held our faith.

THIS EVENING

This evening's Armenian meal that you
cooked with pine nuts and strange
spices unknown to me, helped carry me
over from the food of my family to the
food of yours—the gentle journey a man
makes when he takes a wife: and afterwards
you drew me for the first time. Squinting
beautifully for perspective and giving
me a new glimpse into the changing beauty
caused by our growing love, as my own
severe pose for you gave you a new look
into an aspect of my character you said
you had never seen before.

THE PORTRAITS

The plants are breathing as you work.
On each side of the ones that hang
from the ceiling and rest on the sill
are two early portraits you did in
oils from a time before I was ever
here. Sitting in quiet, my back to
you as you work at your table, I slowly
begin to focus all the parts of your
life into a gentle music that travels
before my eyes from out of my ears,
and that is being punctuated by the
scratchings you make on paper as you
begin a new drawing from out of your
own evolving sphere.

25

YOU AND I AND THE BROTHERS GRIMM

It's noon now and you have gone out
for sandwiches, leaving me alone with
the presence of you that will soon begin
to emerge from this paper as I write.
Last night, after long absence, I returned
again and ate with you the food you had
prepared in the hope that it was being
made for the two of us, and then we went
to bed early and knew fully for the first
time the ecstasy that uniting brings, when
the body, holding its breath in wait,
exhales its love each to each, and then
rising from that glow while I slept, you
made your last drawing for your book from
Grimm, which I am looking at now for the
first time: a wedding scene in which the
bride holds in her heart the ecstasy of
our hour, while her face tells the fictive
tale of another's art. But only you and I
know that the crooked nose above the
mustache of the man wearing a crown—as
he looks down on her protectively from
above—belongs to the man in the bed you
had then just come from.

THE TIME AHEAD

It has taken all this time to accept
the new emotions our love has called up:
to meet the fear we have tried to avoid
of an interfering world—and then,
finally, to move ourselves out of each
other and to travel back together again
(in a singular motion) towards some
unknown but awaiting end—that has
finally given way to this evening's
quiet hour, to the beat of its own
normal and unprepossessing demands.

And so, come 5:30, I sit here and write
and smell the same aroma I have known
from all the years going back, and I
know there will be pilaf and eggplant
from my new girl, who has taken over
from where our earlier lives had come
to an end.

GETTING MARRIED

Walking across Third Avenue, up from the
subway, and on our way home from the
license bureau and the tensions of
that and the day, we moved along
without speaking while you held tightly
to my waist, because you felt yourself
drifting away out of worry and fright.
And staring into your eyes when I knew
they could not focus on mine, I
deliberately shouted, "Getting married,"
to startle you because I knew it would
make you jump—and the look you gave
I have kept, because it carried up from
all the gone years your innocent youth,
and told me in a flash all that I had won.

THE SUBWAY ENCOUNTER

I'm just remembering that coming home on
the subway yesterday afternoon from the
license bureau, I saw our images—for the
first time as a couple—on the window
across from where we sat. The shock of
the upcoming marriage had made you pensive,
caused you to withdraw, and you had a
strangely childlike look, despite your
greying hair and worried look—while I
had the typical open-eyed, immovable
stare of a man in shock. Still, I was
able to look at us as a pair: or rather,
I could feel myself looking at the strange
Armenian couple in the window across from
us and was able to consider them something
other than strangers. But we not only did
not look like us at the moment, or like
a pair, a couple or a match—or anything
else that suggested mutual movement,
accord, or travelers in time. But then
we are not the branded or the damned (as
so many couples who look like couples are),
but two strangers, who became friends and
then lovers—just these happy, frightened,
pleased to do time together, misplaced
Armenians in a strangely foreign land.

THE MARRIAGE DAY

The marriage day has come and now is
nearly gone. From the start it scuttled
along like the subway that took us to
City Hall, all out of whack with the
rhythms we had come to know and rely
upon as our own. Barbara, our witness,
brought a rose, that now sits a stranger
among your simple green plants, and
your lawyer sent champagne which we
had with dinner instead of one of the
wines we like. And then we addressed
our poem/drawing wedding announcements,
and now I will go out to mail them
while you stay home to do the dishes.
But something has been seized and
carried from out of this hour—we can
go forward now as ourselves, for
ourselves, and tomorrow the first leg
of our long journey begins, when we
leave this city and begin in another
place our own quiet country lives.

NEW HAMPSHIRE

Before leaving New York I made Nonny my art director for *Ararat* magazine. She had been an art director at Holt and then at Scribner's, so it was natural for her to design her own children's books, as she would later my books. She changed the face of *Ararat*, both with her outstanding design, and also with her frequent illustrations. I wanted to revolutionize the journal, and the first step in that direction was to bring out a special issue, and the very first from Armenia. Then, for another first, we did a special issue from California, and soon after we drove to Chicago to meet with Arshile Gorky's sister and nephew, for a special issue on Gorky.

While in Armenia we had dinner one evening at the home of the famous artist Kochar, who was best known for his sculpture of DAVID OF SASSOUN. He read my hand at the close of our visit and advised me in urgent tones to return to America, because, he said, I had important work to do. At that point I had only published two books. In time I would wonder if he had not seen that I would someday do a re-telling of the 9th Century Armenian epic, DAVID OF SAS-SOUN.

We didn't realize when we moved to New Hampshire, that this would be the start of countless peregrinations over forty-nine years, earning us the name Gypsy by our friends. Here, in New England we got our first cat, and where Nonny took her ini-tial turn at gardening, which soon became her pas-sion, along with cooking, both of which, although holding a place different from her art, were also deeply sourced in her spiritual nature.

The engine for all of this and more was our growing marriage: our two pillars that made one column, by expanding and feeding our evolving individualities.

We soon bought a station wagon, along with a row boat that could fit in back, and often during the summer months, we would go fishing on nearby Moose Lake, returning home to cook our catch for an early evening supper, often by candlelight. Our bucolic life began immediately to reflect itself in our art, both in spirit and subject matter. Our home was the last house before the Appalachian Trail, and we enjoyed seeing, and sometimes chatting with hikers as they passed by our wide lawn, before disappearing into the waiting wilderness. Our isolation, with welcoming voices in nature speaking intimately to us, seemed the perfect way to begin our marriage.

It was here, in Lyme Center, and in our first home that we began the tradition of sending annual Christmas cards to friends, family, and colleagues, combining new drawings and Christmas poems for the occasion, the art produced by hand from Nonny's linoleum and woodcuts.

WINTER NEW HAMPSHIRE

1/

chickadees
round suet balls and
winter has come

2/

late day
sun sets
on moose mountain
dark cold
blue sky
deer are moving
on evening's
quiet shoulders

shadowless earth

invisible Orion
in the sky

3/

birds in suet
sad wintry song
late day
snow banks the
apple trees
haze down
moose mountain
december fog
drifts
by our window
into sight

4/

snow clouds
slowly lift
off moose mountain

the powdery
snow in their
wake
dust the pines
above the meadow

everything
in all directions
green white brown

5/

white plains
in forest grove
snowshoe tracks
round
pine trees
pass & go

dog barks
off further
hills
echo us home

6/

early morning
snow shadows
blue
clouds bank
the sun
on moose mountain
deer tracks
lead away
& into
our life

THE SECOND POEM

Outside
cats are jumping
from real or
imagined butterfly
shadows—
birds circling
suet balls
are spooked
by their own
motion and
fiery appetites

Inside
hushed motionless
I believe
again in the
salvation of
my poetry
and write

WAITING FOR BIRDS

two day old
seed-filled bird
feeder
hanging from
the porch—
having birds come
fills our home
with what is
outside
our home
as much
a part of our lives
as the furniture
we sit in
food we eat
books we write
waiting
waiting for the birds to come

THE POEM

I am engaged
in making
such books
these poems
for my wife
& life
our animals
and home

moose mountain
& bear hill
before and
in back
tomorrow &
the days gone

I am rescuing
the years
and who will say
that this
obscurity
is not my joy
that I should
not be content
to make such
forms
from out of this
borrowed life

AFTER SUPPER

a little cognac
after supper
in the comfy chair
with Nonny
lying easy
on the couch
Sato sprawled
across her lap
while mongoose nose
rabbit back ears
Bujo
bites her toes
& growls

THE KISS

Bujo
with his big
fat buddha belly
runs across the
room
stops
and kisses Sato
by touching his
nose to hers

and sniffing

what should
I guess it
means
nothing
I am here
it just happened
it is a
small happiness

cup your hands
they will hold
this poem

HEY NONNY

the chickadee
most have seen
a seed
in the snow
down
from the branch
to go neck
deep into the
soft white
of it
& now
the snow is
falling
on his head

THE ROBYS

A family of four
walking up the
path beyond our
house
David is pulling
his son on a sled
Barbara in back
is calling to Jennifer
up in front
they are many colors
the snow is white
the background trees
are green & brown
lips and branches
legs and arms
are moving
from our invisible
window
their voices do
not make a sound

THE ONLY SUN WE'VE SEEN ALL DAY

the messenger gold
beak of the male
grosbeak
beneath the pines
& the downy dust-
brown female grosbeak
at his side
all around them & through
the day it snowed
and all day we waited
at the window
in confusion & want

24:II:72

pushing heavy
breasted through
the snow
hurriedly pecking
at fallen seeds
he makes a
zigzag trail through
the half-buried
prickly pine

now
looking up
he's gone
the only ruby–
crowned kinglet
this winter
hurrah!

26:III:72

early evening
late supper
on the stove
I lay waiting
on the couch
reading Reznikoff
about an earlier
America and
his Israel of
fact & fiction
on the porch
the unnamed raccoon
eats his way
across a dish
of crumbs

13:IV:72

April winter
mud/
white &
bone chill
we stop in
tire track ankle
water hollow
to hear first
bear hoots
of spring

20:XII:72

stillness
snowfall
in the valley
across the mountain
a bird flies
in the cathedral
of the wind

STARTING OUT

the crouch   the wiggle
slowly slowly slowly
swiftly the sprung leap
into forgetfulness
the absent look   the
sidelong glance at nothing
and the mad backward two-step
into a new game of feisty

OPENING THE DOOR
ON THE 18TH OF JANUARY
LATE IN THE EVENING,
TO LET THE CAT IN

as the moon glides thru
streaking clouds

the cat with frightened
tail
sniffs & enters
his only home

CAT & WIFE

Holding the basket on your lap
you shake a packet of
Burpee seeds, while I answer
from the across the room—
"an audience of one"
for Missak has moved from
my chair to yours,
involved now in this
new noise and play,
as you ready spring
in midwinter,
summer plans in your head,
winter out the door.

READING A BOOK, ETC.

reading a book
late at night
winter
waiting for spring
to arrive
I glance up at Nonny
& begin to picture
us in our summer
garden—
seed catalogs
on the floor,
fire burning hotly
in the grate—
and I push our growing
age against
those spring green
garden thoughts
& know that our
eternal moment
is not now
but then
not writing this
furiously waiting
but seed & shovel
in hand
greeting the
new earth
our final comfort
and friend

26:VIII:73

the grasshopper
that leapt into the
snow-on-the-mountain
chased the white
moth out

ALONE

staring at
the empty shoes,
one cocked
over the other
below the
sleeping cat—
I look up:
she's not here
but in the kitchen
making bread
in stocking
feet

THE CONTEST

You are drawing the great
fantasy childhood book
neither of us ever saw,
from out of our own early
wandering-wondering-imaginations;
beautiful, sensual colors;
robes, ouds & dumbegs,
mixed with the flowing
action of robbers & rewards,
none of it real, all of it
more than real; a woman,
two lovers (both bandits)
ignorant of her double life;
horses, jezvehs, samovars & camels,
choruses of colors; and through
it all the children within us
dancing with wide-eyed dazed
amazement and regard.

MORE OF THE SAME

Nonny, with her seeds to
seedling book on her lap,
sits in her chair of knowing,
looks up provocatively,
clasps her hands behind
her head
& gives me pointers
on how all of it
is to be done—
come summer, come
garden time,
when the literary organic
growing lessons
become reality
& we move out of the
comfortable chambers
of learning
& back into the sunshine
of growth & coming life.

4:I:74

Writing on the tear sheet
of the local health food store—
a poem of quiet to the fireplace;
the cat on the bed, Nonny at the
window; while snow and the
dust of time surrounds the
neighborhood and our lives.

ALMOST

the woodpecker
hammers
on the
lilac bush
out for
branch lice
gnats & goodies
at the end
of winter
beside the
abandoned feeder:
the soft colors
in the air
and on the way

ANNIVERSARY SONG

We have worked too hard, and
strained too hard to live this life—
illness has grown out of our
strength—to persist has sometimes
taxed our will to go on.

Now, having given over to our age,
our frailty and the coming tide
(still yet the years will swell)
we return again to the unfolding hour
to make again each act of art, our
talk, the quiet walk in the dark—
the moon—and the fixed hours of rise
and movement and rest.

Thus it has happened we arrive
again and again to each other
with two years added to our
brows, and bow with moving
to our life.

22:IV:73

A touch of yellow mixed
with green, a hint of
purple below red-brown
bursting buds of leaves
against the grey black
bark of forest trees—
and in the distance, slowly
across the land, the sound
of many birds, just arrived,
calling, crying, throwing
their voices against the
sky, against the land.

FROM THE WINDOW

There is something beautiful
out there beyond the window
beyond the growing lawn—
Nonny walking, brooding
thru the yard, returning
her thoughts to the earth
and bringing to my own mind
the fruits of another summer
garden—on the blazing tips
of another summer sun—
and Missak frolicking & dancing
at her hesitant heel
the three winds of the family
with all the elements in moving
conjunction, caught in a drama
only I can see . . . and we are
all atmosphere . . . I, shimmering
at the window (dazed by love),
watching Nonny kneeling on the
new sod—and Missak, suddenly
still, turns & looks beyond,
beyond grass & woods & home,
attuned to his other secret life.

16:IV:73

Missak on his
rocktop moss
covered throne
(in our fern &
flower garden)
sits & catches
flies and keeps
his belly warm

26:VIII:73

the grasshopper
that leaped into the
snow-on-the-mountain
chased the white
moth out

IN THE TRADITION

My family, my wife says,
is all that is important
to me, and saying that
she turns and gives her
full attention to the toll—
house cookies that will soon
emerge from the batter
being beaten by the mixer
that frightens the cat.

And so, the three of us are
in the kitchen, 11:15 P.M.—
a late night drink for me,
a mild fright for the cat,
and cookies for my wife.

Family enough or not, this
is who we are, where we live
and how it is done. It is
part of the formula of life,
and keeping it good and simple
in a poem helps to give pre-
eminence to life. Give thanks
to my wife.

26:VIII:73

the grasshopper
that leaped into the
snow-on-the-mountain
chased the white
moth out

A LETTER FROM THE MUSE

After a long heat steaming
from damp earth morning,
that followed a night of
intermittent rain—along
comes an afternoon breeze
to blow it all away.

Too hot to move in the morning
too rested to care by afternoon,
I sit and wait for the cat to
know I am ready—

comes and sits on my lap and
purrs me this poem.

POEM FOR CATS

If I talk sweetly to Anoush
she immediately purrs moves
her head to one side & asks
to be loved—while Missak
across the porch
rolls over seductively & says,
with his one cat sound
do it too to me

ONIONS FROM NEW HAMPSHIRE

Nonny, in her beets
and celery garden—
gone to seed to woodchuck
to rain and bugs—
brings in her only harvest,
immature but bone-white
immaculate onions
with gangly green stems,
and asks that I bend
to her will and theirs
and bind them top and bottom
in plastic bags—
to carry to our new home;
their tears our only sorrow,
their food our only salvage
from the droopy dog days
of this summer gone.

COLUMBIA COUNTY, NEW YORK

Our pattern of restlessness first asserted itself in New Hampshire, when we decided that a change of scene was needed. So we moved to a place where Nonny had friends, and where she had once been tempted in her single days to buy a home. It would prove to have a long lasting hold on us—ever leaving for something new, but then returning for a life style that suited us in many ways. We bought and sold five homes there in different hamlets over many years: Malden Bridge, New Concord, East Chatham, and Spencertown (twice), with our fondest home in New Concord, situated on twenty-five acres, where we put in a pond, and a large bricked garden.

THE TOY SOLDIER

A toy like the one I played with as a child
is in the antique shop down the street—
the brown soldier, arm still poised,
hand grenade in hand

He never threw it . . . the game went on
I kept him in a box with others
and shared my game with friends.

Such friends they were, my toys, so
trusting was I of the fun, but now
I cannot take this soldier home again
(my own soldiers lost and gone) . . .

Only $3 says the tag that dangles from his head
but I fear his poised arm has already fallen
and our gentle hearts are dead.

PIGEONS

Because we have cut down
the dying elm tree
where they cooed
they fly higher
travel in fewer numbers
glide in the blue sky
less afraid
closer to the great thunderer
their god

VICTIMS 3   CAT O

Missak is dancing
beyond the barn—
a little early
spring voodoo
for the baby squirrels
mice and chipmunks
that will not come

OPENING THE DOOR AND ENTERING THE YARD

I see first
the cock
then the 5 hens
coming,
head-high in the uncut
grass—

my little redheads

NOW

If the cat hunches
    all the way
        to the floor
to have a better look
    at the
        crackling fire—
his nose not six inches
    from the
        growing heat

And if Nonny is stirring
    chili in the kitchen pot
will this be enough
    to make a watcher
        of me—

And noticing
    Missak (listening to her
and remembering myself)
    will I be able
        to ponder
    and see and
say that I have lived—
    claiming it all
        in this trembling poem

For if I do not
        who will come after
and say that
        this place
                has been a
place before
        and who will
                master the rite
if we fail to catch
        the magic at its source

which is and is and is:
the rhythm
        of the heartbeat
                in love with time

CHRISTMAS EVE

Christmas eve and the mind quiets:
empty the days ahead
the days behind

I look inside my shell
and see the mirror of my heart

What do I know, what do I want:
to be here in all my presence,
neither seeking nor asking;
only this, myself, quietly
breathing the breath
of my quiet life

EARLY SPRING

Our chickens are
being shadowed by
a lone pigeon   out
for our store bought
corn   months before
the season

He sits on the barn top
—a new corner—
hesitates to enter
their coop   uncertain
if this is news that
will travel well
be believed back home

MANHATTAN

Flashback: In the time just before accepting the *Ararat* editorship, while staying with friends in Lenox, Massachusetts, I wrote LOOKING OVER HILLS. I had been instantly enthralled by the enchanting beauty and serenity of the Berkshires. Of the poems I wrote then, I would later write: There was a declaration behind the vision that produced the poems, which were poems about the invisible, interconnected fabric of the universe and life, and what I not only sensed but knew, was this: I had become a channel, a radio that could transmit messages between stations, but this glory was not and is not mine, it is a temporary state, and I knew that nothing of its quality would accrue to me if I were to leave it at that; that is, if I accepted this gift but did not take a step beyond, and move into a dimension where I could make something that is mine, and that will not, cannot be taken away.

It was around this time that my growing interest in Gurdjieff was coming into fruition, leading us to begin our long search together for a group to study with, that would lead to our joining the Gurdjieff Foundation in New York.

Nonny had been slow to warm up to my spiritual search, which had begun for me with my recent reading of Carlos Castaneda's first book; Nonny to feel that having at last found her mate, and with a settled country life, her happiness was now complete—while this quest for a spiritual life, with its search for self-knowledge and growth in Being, seemed to her to be a threat to our marriage. I was slow to introduce her to some of the literature, but

when she starting reading Gurdjieff's opus, ALL & EV-
ERYTHING, changed for her. She came to later realize
that it was while in New Hampshire, during our first
year of marriage, she came down with breast cancer
that resulted in a mastectomy.

As she came back into conscious following
the surgery, her hand went instantly to her chest, and
a voice inside her said, "*This is not what your life is
about.*"

After endless readings of books by and about
Gurdjieff, we had to accept that if we were to con-
tinue with our studies and engagement in the The
Work, as Gurdjieff's teaching came to be called, we
would have to find a group; but since both of us
were loners and solitary artists, the idea of joining
something / anything was repugnant to us, feeling
we would lose more than we stood to gain, should
we make a dramatic change in our way of life. One
day, reading a book by Gurdjieff, I walked into the
kitchen where Nonny was preparing dinner, and sat
at the kitchen table to stare out the window—when
above my head in the vast distance, Gurdjieff's head
appeared, and absent a voice, said to me, "It will be
all right." Just that, said once, and instantly I knew
that we needed to find a group to study with as soon
as possible.

Our resistance had now completely vanished.
We quickly located and checked out two different
groups in the East, but they were clearly wrong for
us; when my sister, who had studied with one of
Gurdjieff's "disciples," J. G. Bennett, recommended

that we call the Gurdjieff Foundation in Manhattan. We were instantly taken in and welcomed by the director, Lord Pentland. After renting our home, we moved into one of the apartments on Third Avenue in Manhattan, and began attending weekly talks on the teaching. In a short time we were put in a group. It wasn't long, however, before we became disappointed with the teaching as offered there, which was theoretical, head oriented and without heart, making it very wrong for us, But of Gurdjieff, the Master, we had no doubt. The future seemed uncertain, but we had struck our first do in the Work octave, and our lives as it turned out, would be changed forever.

The electrifying energy of New York had a profound effect on my writing life, and almost instantly I began writing the poems that would appear in my next book, TAKING THE SOUNDINGS ON THIRD AVENUE. Like so many during this period, we believed that country living was the best answer to the freedom we were seeking in opposition to the disorder during that turbulent time the country was angrily going through. New York appealed to my temperament, and looking back now at the various poems comprising that book, I was surprised but shouldn't have been, because nature was the overriding voice and vision that drove those poems.

TAKING THE SOUNDINGS
ON THIRD AVENUE

O the Avenue
        hums
Chrysler, Empire State
and you too of the
        golden dome
Towers tall, towers to fall
        O even towers not yet born
Cast your shadows
        but do not come

◊

The STANDPIPE
        painted all or
        in part (green,
        red, yellow or
        black), or often
        of polished brass—
Beside the metal grating,
        or quiet, alone, erect,
Or pushing manly out of
        polished facade,
        on this or any other
        street in Manhattan:
Commands, by its perfect
        realization, our own
        attention & energy—
For, when focused, they become for us

the center of a composition
of a tireless work of art
of endless variations and
possibilities, that
never wear out

◊

At Cassaro Bros. Food Market
neatly arranged
in their boxes,
all the colored
fruits
from this & other lands

◊

the Armenian grocer
starting out the window
sees the old country

◊

the drunk in the
doorway stops his
right hand—paper sack
muscatel—half-way up

as left hand rises
to my passing
"uh, quarter please"

right hand finishes
the important gesture—
drinks

◊

the country cat
at the tenement
window, sniffs
the noises and
alarms—stares
out the window
expressionless,
his tail anchored
to another sound

◊

the grey wing
beat of silence
in my lap—
pigeons overhead

◊

the new november wind
is blowing summer
out to sea

◊

A halo of silence
just brushed past me
on the sidewalk
A Peruvian Indian couple
with the jungle still
in their hair

The couple that walked
by, walked back,
and the man stretched
to his fullest height
to pick a sprig of berries
from the overhanging tree
at 210 E. 26 St (around the
corner of 3rd Avenue)
which brought a smile to
the woman's face, that
broadened when she looked
into the green & flowering
courtyard of the Maltese
Super and his wife;
and turning to take
the sprig of hawthorne
she gave him her smile
and turned with the sprig
that shone now on them too

As the day surrenders its
meaning to the night,
lights come on and blink
a new hello—
and we are at the
Portuguese Restaurant
(Lexington & 28th St)
where everything becomes
quiet with an inner
stillness that goes
with the night and
the people, under a
completed moon,
Fado on the
phonograph,
that sings
of yester-
day as if
tomorrow
shall
never
come

◊

Not a burnt candle on a shrine
But an empty wine bottle in the doorway

◊

The hidden foot
dancing
finds the earth that prays

◊

Every time I pass by
Cassaro's Market
I start thinking of
the fast buck:
Figs, 49 cents each
Persimmons, 2 for 39
Pomegranates, 59 cents each
Sometimes it costs more
to be Armenian than
it's worth

◊

the beat of pigeon
wings and feet,
taxi horn and gust
of smoke, all curl,
fly and swirl past
the sleeping drunk,
who is bent too
in a posture of flight

◊

the hawthorne berries
must be ripe—
5 pigeons on the
sidewalk, pecking
4 sparrows in the
branches, knocking
them down

◊

A Thanksgiving shower washes
the streets—making warm puddles
that muffle all sound—taxis
have stopped their horns—the
people still here are hurrying
home—pumpkin pie bakeries have
turned on their lights—and just

as I turn the corner for home
a heavy-breasted woman leans out
her window—stares at the new old
city she loves

◊

gliding with the tide
the barge is pulling
a piece of the city
out to sea

◊

the wing-set lone seagull
floating in the sky
takes the city's pulse

◊

five doves of autumn
blow past the
naked chestnut tree
seeking a hidden
bower

◊

the birds are chirping
as never before—
(on the other side of
our drawn shades—

a farewell note to the
departing mourners,
who are carrying our
neighbor's belongings
away

◊

sparrows in the trees
seagulls overhead—

where are the crows
of silence—the
cardinals of song—
the thrush that once
sang me into wakefulness
from its faraway bed

◊

Just this:

　　3 sparrows

pecking at the new seeds
beneath our courtyard tree
were so tamed by hunger,
that when I reached to
touch one, I nearly did

◊

the Japanese painter
on the third floor
practices her flute:

the sound drifts across
the Avenue and returns,
suffused with the miracle
　　and melancholy
　　of the night

◊

The clean & orderly Korean
fish and fruit peddlers—
side by side—between 25th
& 24th Streets:

    push their children to
speak—misspell the names
of things—laugh self-consciously,
showing many teeth—
hurry & wait—have
the look in their eyes of
two countries going at
once—

Are doing all the business
on the block.

◊

The Sabrette vendor
    singing Hungarian
    under his breath
Lifts up his head
    (as I pass)
    winks, nods,

    and the beat goes on

◊

Dogs on a leash—
dogs in the street—
cats in the windows
and parakeets in a cage

and now, suddenly, this
stranger, the hamster
of my childhood, coming
(in a cage),
hoisted by two Puerto
Rican lads of 9 & 10,
or thereabouts.
the woman who just walked
into the garbage cans,
gave them an indignant swipe—

another of the eccentric or
blind ones

◊

wind rips thru the
belly of the city,
announces a coming time—
and suddenly everything
turns another way:
even the pigeons have
a further look,
as if their wings were mercy
and could beat such time away

◊

held for an instant
in the taxi's passing
lights—two drunks in
an archway—one with
hardened, mangled face,
and the other, younger,
with a bottle paper-bagged,
tapping a shivering leg

◊

stepping gingerly over
the new puddles (of an
overnight winter squall)
I pass huge buildings
without looking up

all held fast for the
moment in depressions
that hold the rain
that hold the light
of buildings
far far up

◊

In the autumn-come-winter park
the grey squirrel with perky ears
displays a perfect hazel nut—
a gift, obviously, not of these trees.

And makes a splendid show of burying
his treasure, by reshuffling the
leaves & scratching the grey ground.

Then, exhausting that instinctive
impulse or pleasure, eats the nut
in hand, waves his tail, sits up
neatly, and hurries along and waits,
for the next soft touch to come along.

◊

the ancient dog and lady
are pulling each other
along on a single leash.
First he tugs for the
curb, to sniff whatever
is there: litter can,
mailbox, telephone pole—

then she pulls towards the
middle of the sidewalk, to be
nearer the people walking by,
and, as I pass, she
first eyeballs me hard
then   S N I F F S

the block garden
sitting dusty & enclosed
by threatened tenements
on all sides,
          manages to push
forth what it grows:
scarecrow (even) to one
side—to ward off nothing,
to welcome drunks (under
its hat I sense a bottle
of port)—before a mural
of the garden against the
brick building that faces
the garden:

for here where
everything is not enough,
in a place where anything at all
is often too much, and
nothing you choose is apt
to remain: have me, the
mural says, once in your
mind and once in my
heart
          citizens, pass by

THREE POEMS

30:XII:75

O quiet misty
rain   black
cat damp and
hungry for love

his motor
turns over
in my idle lap
and hums . . .

31:XII:75

the white daisies
above the sleeping cat
inhale the night

3:I:76

a beer, a cigarette,
(for Nonny's gone to town)

Missak, a new quiet
(and rain all around)

A man without a woman
is a very lonely sound

ROWAN

Of another's name
    your grandfather's:
                you are Ronny
to us—
    a sweet flower
            turning your face
everywhere
    to be loved
In this orchid
    of a room   we call hope
you buzz
    around me
            once twice
and alight—
    hiding a haunting
            sadness
with a gentle heart
            I hold you
    protectively
with my thoughts
            my words
and let you go—
 You ask what kind of
    poems
            I write
I write this kind

TO NONNY

It is the afterglow of dinner
on your face—
new tablecloths and candles;
in another setting, in another
town—
that suddenly brings forward
new talk of old failures:
of life unspent, of opportunities
gone:

And it is this, this new
discovery of self,
swift and silent (even in speech) un-
diminished by the hour or year:
your being that I suddenly
see again
and love.

CHRISTMAS EVE

Christmas Eve and the mind quiets:
empty the days ahead
the days behind

I look inside my shell
and see the mirror of my heart

What do I know, what do I want:
to be here in all my presence,
neither seeking nor asking;
only this, myself, quietly
breathing the breath
of my only life

AURORA, OREGON

During our near two years at the Foundation we began a friendship with Betty Deran, and it was to her we turned after walking out on the Foundation. She had left the Foundation for a short period to study with a group in Oregon, and then later returned. Apparently she had left her heart in Oregon (but soon to return) and encouraged us to meet the teacher who founded the group there, Annie Lou Staveley, whose teacher had been Jane Heap, a major figure in the Work, close to Gurdjieff, who had directed her to teach his work in London, which is where our soon-to-be teacher, Annie Lou Staveley who had been a student in Jane Heap's earliest group, with Jane taking them frequently to Paris for meetings with Gurdjieff.

Mrs. Staveley's group had purchased a plot of land near the township of Aurora, Oregon. Her group was comprised largely of young people a full generation younger than us, whose parents were roughly our age. Being malleable and unfixed, they were loose enough to be a decent fit for us, and in time we came to think of them as family. We remained there for nine years, converting a large hop barn for living quarters, where we started a small press to serve the Work, teaching ourselves and our crew to handset type, print by letterpress, and bind books by hand in limited editions, while also helping to revive the ancient art of marbling. Before long we began to publish books on and about the Work, including three volumes of my poems on the daily life of The Farm. Years later I wrote of our time there in my book, ON A SPACESHIP WITH BEELZEBUB: BY A GRANDSON OF GURDJIEff, the subtitle referencing the grandson in Gurdjieff's opus, being the generation he was writing his book for, and we were of that generation.

SUNDAY, EARLY

The dog called Bear
is sleeping in front
of the frosty kitchen doors
where the misty cooks
are breathing their steam
into the bread that rises
with their breath
to the dining hall above

Where one of us, myself,
lazily looks out the window
to see the dog called Jessie
running weed-high and happy
to bring the first untested news
of the early Sunday day.

MARY JANE

Thank you for being there
munching on grass
beside the new school

with your young pudding face
your nose full of flies
and your funny little horns

it is right that you are there
just there on your pallet of straw
where you greet the children

each morning as they arrive,
it is almost as if you were never away
your moo the moon

the new month of April
opening our eyes
to all the possibilities of love

EARLY SUNDAY

It is the sight of a woman
   feeding chickens
   that causes a man to
   remember again what
   came to him once
   long before words
   long before the first written poem
For in seeing her there
   he knows again all form
   and motion,
   and the rhythm and sequence
   of time:
but the lugubrious poet must write.
   He must write because,
   being a man who wishes words
   to accompany living time
   he will have his poem—
   and so he writes:
The early morning maid
   on the farm
   with dew in her hair
   and a bowl in her circling arm
   is throwing seeds
   in nets of spray
   to the chickens
   that have gathered round.
When the scene becomes the absence
   of the scene it was
   and only its ambience remains

He quietly walks to the hen house
    to see there dainty in
    a feminine hand.

    Shhh baby checks inside
        QUIET PLEASE

There is a beauty in all this
    beyond the telling

IN THE GRENHOUSE
for Nonny

In the seeds in her
      hands
all memory of life and growth and
      death
is held in whirling motion—

and now
      as her cupped hands move
      she begins to feel the canopy
      of heaven turn above her shoulder
while slowly she tucks her tiny
      stars of remembrance
back into the earth from whence
      they have come—
feeling their burnished thoughts
      bloom in her head

I RIDE THE RED TRACTOR

I ride the red tractor
    across the green earth
The host of starlings
    who purple come
Fearless at last of this
    human form—
And we are suddenly arm-extended
    wing-beat abreast,
And suspended, joyous, I am being
    churned across the earth—
The far-flung hope of some distant hand.

O if I could only be to bird and animal
    red tractor or green
And come with them at will
    across this vibrant, mysterious land
Rejoicing in the food
    revealed by each turning tread
And they secure in the halo of my love—
    this is all of holiness I would be,
And to the rhythm of wing-beat
    and animal tread we would move
Across the golden face of day,
    into the rosy back of night.

EASTER MORNING

The absolute stillness of 6 A. M.
Only the smoke rising from the barn
where the women are preparing breakfast.
The grey clouds are again themselves,
but they move with such quiet at this hour
that only they know they are there.
The sun is far away
and we are far away from the sun.
The blackbirds that have been with us
for so long now
that they are a part of us
just flew in a cluster
into and out of my sight.
They are a comfort and will fill
a small wound.
I am told the children will hunt
for Easter eggs after breakfast.
That is good. I do not know what
it means but it is good.
While new ceremonies are being born
old ones are quietly dying out.
Soon the cars will be arriving
and with them the wings of other voices,
but now it is quiet, unearthly quiet,
only the swift and intermittent black
birds, the clouds like smoke, and
the smoke an earthly cloud.
The day of death may not be unlike
this moment now—when one is helplessly

alone and glad to be, unable not to be ready
for the entrance of the next experience,
which may be the last, or only the last of its kind.

I have to remember that it is Easter
and try to realize again what that means

EASTER EVENING

You look up and the trees are all at once green.
It takes all day to stop and look
and then suddenly the sky is all its one color:
clear, in that color that is no color,
the color of quiet evening—
the evening color of the sky in spring:
and there, far off on the wide horizon,
is a rosy glow, the glow of evening,
the rosy substance of spring;
and below that, at the point
from which this poem and remembrance begins,
are the green leaves that have suddenly
come home to summer;
the occasion of the lives of trees
having begun
exactly and as always
perfectly to the beat of celestial time
and earthly time
reminding us now at Easter
what it means for us
to make our own lives.

TO THE MAN OR WOMAN WHO BROUGHT
THEIR MEDITATION CUSHION TO THE TOP
OF THE BARN AND LEFT IT THERE, ALLOWING
ME TO IMAGINE YOUR VANISHED BUT LIVING
PRESENCE AN HOUR OR TWO LATER WHEN I
CAME TO DO MY WORK

Thank you, I used it
while shelling corn—
leaving it where I
last sat during the
actualization of my work.

When you found it Monday
and returned to your spot,
did you feel the work I
put into it the day before,
and did you wonder to yourself
if I felt the work
you had left in it all the mornings before that?

We want to touch everything
in this manner, with all
parts of our bodies, consciously,
with all our feelings and thoughts,
intentionally,
for it is in this way
that we are trying to
awaken to The Farm
as heart

115

RENEE

I visit the little school
　warm my chilled back
　against the hot wood stove,
　and sit on a far cushion,
　hoping not to be seen—
And watch the scene unfold,
　naturally, in its easy,
　everyday way—
And slowly, one by one, they
　come and show me what
　they do, and ask that
　I button their smocks
Or they just tell me their
　names, and ask me mine.
One of the teachers' name is
　Judy, the other is Mr. Smyth,
　for everyone here
　has taken the name
　they wish to be called by—
There is Gottlieb, Erin and Vance;
　Tasha and Kirsten and Matt;
　Alfred and Aubrey and Leo;
　to mention only a few,
Finally, the pixie of the crowd—
　always, every gathering of souls
　must have one that is the most
　vivacious of the lot—
Comes and jumps into my arms,
　unconcerned over the restraint

and caution and quiet that
contains the rest—
You are my outdoor elevator,
    I tell her—which floor
    shall it be—but she only
    giggles and falls backwards,
    while I hang onto her knees—
This one used to be Mona,
    Mr. Smyth says, but she
    decided to be reborn, and
    that's what her new name means—
That's right, that's right,
    formerly Mona says,
    my name is Renee.
Maybe, I think, the school itself
    should have been called that:
    it seems that kind of place.
When the time comes to leave
    I ease out the way I came, unnoticed,
    knowing something,
    something very precious,
    has been kept alive.

CELEBRATING GURDJIEFF'S
ONE HUNDREDTH BIRTHDAY
January 13, 1978 | Aurora, Oregon

The fog lifts, falls,
    is penetrated by invading
    lights of cars.

I imagine candles in procession
    walkers in Asian mountains,
    chanting as they come to prayers.

Here their descendents arrive
    in shields of tin and glass
    over mended gravel roads.

O brothers, our Fathers
    in the distant firmament
    with our drum the silent wheel
    that turns
    and our prayer beads rattling
    in the engine
    that hums under the hood

We   Affirming   Come

THE FAIRY GARDEN

Being careful not to crush
their tiny green heads,
I sit on the raised
brick garden ledge
and face the flowering mounds
of herb garden life.

I have come here at the children's
request, to see as they have
the home of the garden fairy.
And I have come here,
not with their wonder,
but with my own quiet thoughts.

Slowly, I find myself becoming
smaller and smaller, until
I am the size of the purple
flowering herbs beside me,
where white butterflies.
and brown have come.

And bees and moths and
tiny bee-fly insects
that are noiseless, busy, alive—
and suddenly I remember again
as a child, and I understand
what the children have meant.
It is a fairy, all of it is a fairy.

119

For this is the name they have given
to this aspect, to this garden
for the whole of life.

JAPANESE ANEMONES

We are looking at the petals
of pink and white flower,
picked today, and now in a vase
before our eyes—

the vase, that is made of prisms
of glass,
complements and reflects a pink
that is its own that
is in the flower,
that is in us and the day—

and one of us opens a book,
to give a name to the flower,
for we would know how we lived
with a name—

but the name cannot enhance
the fragrance of the hour,
that is named by our presences
that cannot speak of what has been felt
in a day that includes only flowers,
the picking of berries and the breaking
of bread, made this very evening by
our hands—

a conjoining so quiet, that we have
looked to name a flower
because blessedness has been ours
but has no name.

121

IN THE ORCHARD

Passing by the peach tree
I stop, reach up, feel the
peach give in to my pressing
fingers, and pluck it from
the branch that held it in wait
for this hour.

Walking, I wondered at the process
of life, and how delicious it can
be when one is aware of the
present moment and engages totally
in the act of living, in all
its simplicity, wonder and truth.

Just a peach, oozing its life,
and a man, any man, head bent,
intent not to let any of its
secret life spill back into the
ground, easing the pit free,
fully aware of the different tastes
of flesh and skin and fuzz.

AUTUMN

There is a moment at dusk
when the earth exhales its
last breath of day

And time is suspended between
departure and arrival, between
exit and entry, when all

the greening becomes gold,
and the blue bowl of heaven
a mirror that holds itself up

As comforter and complement
as the other half, that is not
better for being higher

But, being higher, looks down on
what is of itself but not itself
and feels the ascension of the lower

Pushing its green branches
of gold skyward, dying again
again being born.

THE CAT

Sossi sits at the top of the new-
made stairs that lead to our
home in the hop barn (finely sanded
wood still to be varnished) that
complement newly-laid tiles on
the floor beneath.

I go and check on her, pregnant lady,
but she doesn't look up at me,
only wags her bushy tail to say:
I'm here, I hear you, I've found
my place, now leave me alone.

And so I look, too, at what she sees
and it is good, it is worth sitting
in front of and slowly taking in.
Through the double-doors below her
(that she faces), the hanging red
lantana plant rolls with the wind—
while the flower garden casts a final
light and color against the coming dark.

Whatever it all means or doesn't mean,
Sossi is in it—she is so completely in it
that she has become its meaning. The thing
seen and the seer have become one.

Humbly I turn and leave what is alone.

TURKEYS

Say it, the tom is all ego and male,
Puffs one second, unpuffs the next.
And what was the cause of his puffing,
and why did he cease?
A cat will leap from a butterfly
shadow sometimes, but he will do so
with humor, enjoying his own fright
in a game he plays for himself
But for the tom it is not even
butterfly shadows.
It is simply, one moment all feathers
and fight, the next minute
nothing—Mr. Nonentity himself.

It's a hell of a life. Consider it!
The fluff and feathers serve no purpose,
and signal his own fear—though he
pretends to be scaring others off—
and his face (that turns blue from fear),
and that silly, flappy foreskin on his face.
Really!—is that what ego is all about?

But then there is the hen, all squawk
and whining sex. Everything, just everything,
is a complaint. Come here, go away (she says
to Tom), get me more, get me less. Why can't you
see what I want. You never can, you never will. Oh,
never mind. . .

it's too late,
and doesn't matter anyhow.

Oh God, the point is clear, why You
have put turkeys here.

HOW YOUR CALF WAS BORN LAST NIGHT

Mary Jane, they say—I think it's the
Chinese—that a picture is worth ten
thousand words; so picture us, dear girl,
looking down at you from the Movements Hall,
your back to us as you faced the end of
the rainbow that looked as if it would bite
your nose—while off in the farther corner
of the same field, the other cows were
huddled, oblivious, just eating grass—

And so there you are, right this minute,
licking your baby bull, just as we knew
you would, you big lump of feminine gorgeousness,
you grass eating doll, you milky, silky babe.

TODAY

The day Rosa the pig arrived into
the pen made by Birkemeier,
the cows huddled by the separating
fence, and mooed so big you knew
it was talk—angry talk!—
because just the night before
a baby bull was born—an absolutely
new experience for everyone—
and last week Jenny the donkey showed up—
and Wow! this is too much, a huge
white pig. But Birkemeier, who was
inside the fence to our outside,
was standing with his arm around Jenny
just taking it all in: a farmer, big,
in command, just happy as grass
about everything that was doing down.

A QUESTION

Why in autumn, when the earth
begins slowly to rest
that I, the poet (and admittedly
the observer)
turn away as other men do
and begin also to search for what
needs to be preserved
and contained
for the time ahead.

The material for observation, it seems,
is lost—
but for the moon in its seasons
and the season's turning tide,
the exhaling and inhaling of one
day into the next,
and the moods and seasons of the heart.

I sigh, unexpectedly, and take up my pen.

AUTUMN

There is a moment at dusk
when the earth exhales its
last breath of day

And time is suspended between
departure and arrival, between
exit and entry, when all

the greening becomes gold,
and the blue bowl of heaven
a mirror that holds itself up

As comforter and complement
as the other half, that is not
better for being higher

But, being higher, looks down on
what is of itself but not itself
and feels the ascension of the lower

Pushing its green branches
of gold skyward, dying again
again being born.

JANUARY 12, 1981

You were in the trees, but when I looked up
you were gone. Later, by the compost heap
you saw me, I guess, but I was unaware and
realized only later that it was you—busy
imperceptible, although not far from my side,

All day you were at your work, and I was
at mine. Raking leaves, weeding, and mowing
the lawn. It was, this day, a busy, early
spring—for this is January and already we
have done all these things.

I even found a dandelion beside a stone in
the rose garden. Because it is January
I should not be surprised to see you there
or be surprised not to see you there;
I have taken you for granted for so long.

Except for the new greens and first gold,
it is still winter and your gray and black
coat says it, says it as if your name were winter,
instead of Junco. Winter bird, there among the
walnut branches, unseen but present, I need

131

To be reminded that soon you will be gone,
for I do not know when I will see you again.
But today we worked this earth together,
you among the new branches, brittle, gray
and leafless, and me among the dormant bushes.

Today, at last I learned your song.

WINTER SOLSTICE
Aurora, Oregon / December 21, 1981

Two by two they proceeded with candles.
Singing into the solstice night

under a moon hidden by darkened clouds,
the night heavy-laden with sorrow

and a civilization gone—

and two followed with candles
to light-en what had been passed

and they felt a movement in the earth
and saw in the shadows the gathering sheep

and other animals moving toward the light—
while we, who would receive the singers
in this ceremony made by us, huddled

under the eaves of the barn, holding
our children on trembling shoulders

waiting for the lights that moved through
the dark, to voices whose gift was the order

of procession and holy witness—
to what could not be known, and could not be told,
but that had already been felt by each of us.

SOSSI

Whenever Sossi sees me outside
our house she turns away
or slinks away. Or hides.
Afraid I might pester her with
love or attention—
or afraid I might call her inside.
Or interfere with her play.

But whenever (and as soon as)
I go into the garden,
here she comes.
And when she is just the right
distance away, she sits down, facing me,
and watches me at my work.

For sometime now I've watched
her watching me in this way.
Until now I had assumed that because
I was down on my knees she felt safe—
or felt assured that I wouldn't pester
her, or take her indoors, etc.

But today, while I was weeding
the flower garden, I noticed her get up—
very intentionally—in order to change
her position, so she could watch me work
from a better vantage point.

Why?

I think, finally, I know.
She cannot work.
In one way she is my superior; and we
both know it.
She is contained and serene
in her being.
She knows her worth.
And she allows me to attend her.
It is an agreement we have come to, naturally.

But then there is this business of work,
and its meaning in our relationship.
She doesn't need to understand it but I do
And today, very simply, I realized that
I can work And she cannot.

While I was watching her today
watching me,
I felt for the first time
a real sense of pity for her
And a real sense of pity for myself
Because I could see she was transfixed
by something I so often try to get out of,
or take for granted. And almost never value.

But by her attention and interest
and fascination (cats are incapable of envy),
she made me see that I was engaged in
something very high.
So high that we do not see it—

135

do not see that it is both our privilege
and our possibility,
and that part of this work is to care
for the lower creatures, who will
cease to be lower—to our higher
the moment we make
this caring also our work.

SUMMER SOLSTICE

Aurora, Oregon / June 21, 1982

We gathered in the early dawn under
the filbert trees and the eaves of the school—
against the drizzling rain,
that seemed at first an intruder;
as if we knew what the day should be

And waited, we did not know for what;
watching the gray, amorphous sky,
and in the distance—the distance we faced
a streak of pink appeared, turned orange
and revealed a breath of light, far far away.

The singers sang to that and the light inside—
ancient songs of praise to the sun and the season,
and the light.

The piano in the schoolyard, covered with an
Oriental rug against the rain, seemed
to say something, we could not tell what—
perhaps about a relationship that existed
long ago between man and nature—
when man knew what it was he wished
to be related to, in ceremonies since lost
and forgotten, that we, now, in our presence
yearned to renew.

The music, scored for our search, accompanied
the dancers in a Movement that seemed written
for the sun. Or was it the wind. Or the rain that,
having abated, began again when the dancers
moved into their places.

And when their arms took the first raised position
we knew that all things join that are related,
and all that is related is one and comes from one,
and must be re-blended again with the source.

And in the wish that was in the faces
of the dancers, we found our own wish
and in it our relationship to God.

THE CAT IN THE TREE

Perched in the cherry tree
high above the herb garden,
Sossi watches Jim Barton at his work.
She is there waiting for my return
(having left during our walk together)
and now she watches as I enter again
and begin talking to Barton.

She watches as if she knew what everything
was for, and why everything is where it is—
she sits on a horizontal board placed in the tree
by the children, and turns her head toward the
children, calling now in the orchard.

It is a timeless moment.
For her there ares only timeless moments.
Slowly the silence in the wonder of everything
surrounds.

THE SILENT KNOWING

From my unusual perch high
up in the soundless barn
I see in the distance

children hurling themselves
in their swings
their voices imagined

but their joy and happiness
known to me
and as real to me as my own

for I know it as I know
the experience of the farmer
(also seen from my window)

as he shovels grain into a wagon
in silence—
the silence of work

that is held in the halo
of making and being
as the children are held

as we all are held
in the blessings of time

MORRIS, NEW YORK

After our nine years on The Farm, the time had come to initiate ourselves by returning to life and making life our teacher, following the example Gurdjieff had drawn in his book, MEETINGS WITH REMARKABLE MEN. In the film made from his book, Gurdjieff is told to remain in the monastery until he acquires a force in himself, that he can measure and test himself with in life.

Returning to Columbia County we searched for a Vandercook Press like the one we had in Oregon, finding an exact model in the western part of the state, where we soon settled and gathered a group to work with. Taking The Farm in Oregon as our example we bought a farm house with acreage, and before long our small group began to attract others.

In our nine year absence from everyday America, life had changed, and the people who came to us now were not interested in the general practice of the Work as much as they were its practical application to their lives. There was nothing really surprising in this, once we took into account that life was slowly, mysteriously evolving on a vast scale, with the various Eastern teachings gradually changing the nature of spirituality in the West, resulting in a more practical application of Work ideas. We could see for ourselves that the Work could very easily become stultified and cultish, which was already happening with the groups we were aware of in different parts of the country.

At the same time we were meeting this challenge I began writing the poems that would complete my cycle of Farm Poems. In advance of this I went through a timeless period where I suffered remorse for all my unconscious actions, where I had been hurtful with cruel words and actions, whether from defensiveness, carelessness, anger, frustration, or negativity. Each and every one of my unconscious actions throughout my life began to appear before me with inescapable clarity, and from which I suffered great remorse. From the grace that made this seeing possible, I was able to use my writing gift to convey in new poems a vision that was seemingly beyond me, yet was mine to record. These poems were a leap beyond the previous poems written on the Farm, where I dealt largely with my situation inside a landscape of people and place that was a given, but this now was a different terrain, both inner and outer, and what I was witnessing was my own troubled and growing soul, untempered by any outside influence, good or bad.

THE SCHOOL

Walking across the lawn from
the front door, dew on my shoes
(the spiders were busy last night
making new webs) I fetch the
morning paper from the box,
one of the daily rituals of life.

For years I didn't read a paper
or anything else not connected
to my search, but now there is
a breathing in the spaces between
push and pull, where pause is not
a rest but a letting go of more
and more of what I am not.

Working with other for a long
time makes a seeing; the acquiring
the denying, the possessing, the
losing. Never suspecting it was
all the same: the confused passage
by which clarity arrives.

Now everything moves in its time.
Life changes every day, and doesn't
change: new, rich, and strange.
And the ideas are one's life, as
given by fate, and one has the will
for the puzzle, the tableau,
the unfenced arena where the
real drama is going on.

THE PRESS AT BUTTERNUT CREEEK

Today I printed, this week I wrote—
the two abiding passions of my life,
one dormant for three, the other denied
for nearly two years—suddenly coming
together at one time. It makes you wonder.

The press—like my old SP 15 Vandercook—
printed beautifully—right off the
bat, as the saying is, and I had been
in terror that it wouldn't print
at all, or poorly, and me not knowing
what to do about it. But like I say:
Perfect! Beautiful! My heart soared!

The other press printed badly the whole
last year I was there—sitting
in a chair I no longer belonged in—
going down as I went down, fading—don't
tell me machines don't have an emotional
life, or at least, that they don't respond
to ours. I used to throw people
out of the press room whom I called wasters,
and instantly the stalled press would roar,
with me right there, roaring with it.

Great God in Heaven! You can't know how happy I am to be printing again. An essay by Gurdjieff—that, when I read it years ago, changed my life—as his ideas were always changing my life—and go on changing it still.

I may have twenty years to go, I may have one, but there is something certain. I'm gong to be writing poems, I'm going to go on printing—to the glory of everything, for the glory of God!

GARDEN II

I can see it now, she said,
we will plant watercress over there,
and mist, rising, will reveal
mint in our little garden
by the broken well
with the spring-running stream
and a tiny pond for goldfish
and waterlilies,
by the close-cropped grass—
over there!

"EVERY FARM HAS A BLUEBIRD"

We imagine these hills in December
that are green now in September,
throughout the long Butternut Valley.

Soon it will be one year we are here,
and we speak to each other as we ride,
of autumn colors and other blessings,
after long exile and recent return.

And whatever we say, home is what
the talk always means. "Every farm
has a bluebird," rings in my head,
her words like a melody I will
ever return to.

THE CAT

Tessie descends the stairs
positions herself between us
on the rug, blinks beguilingly
then falls on her side, resting.

What to do! On one side Nonny
studying books on gardening,
already awaiting spring
and I on the other side,
silently writing.

But she likes it here,
perfect for her or not,
and there is a kind of quiet
hum she hears—so many days
have gone like this,
so many more to come.

The hollow in-breath,
sensed but not seen,
between be and become.

THE GARDEN

There's an area just beyond the door
needs tending

A dip in the land,
and then a rise

and there at the base a garden
walled in, naturally, with a well

no longer in use, a stream
that flows only in spring

brambles, fallen tree limbs, weeds,
brush piles, and an old outhouse

crumbling returning to the ground.

LADIES, CATS

It is a small thing perhaps.
I record it!

Nonny shelling beans
while Tessie, crouched

on the end table beneath the lamp
that lights Nonny's work

steps then withdraws
and steps again into her lap

after the bowl has been removed for her

and now she is all stretched
out the bowl on her blind side

and the paper on the floor
to which Nonny lobs the shells

(over Tessie's head) that
Tessie watches—puzzled,

serene, exactly-perfectly
where she wants to be.

IT'S BEEN

too long since I've seen a bluebird.
Which makes me think they've
gone away, the pair that were here
when we moved in last winter.

only three weeks ago we discovered
their manmade bird house in the grass,
fallen from the fence, its bottom
no longer intact, that I have

since repaired, and the bluebirds
are now before my eyes
but nowhere else, before my eyes
but not in their nest.

FOR THE ONE WHO KNOWS

It bothers us that we don't
know each other.

But realizing this the bother lessens.
Why? It goes elsewhere.

It goes into realizing that we
are speaking across an abyss.

This should bother us
and it does.

Years go by, but it doesn't pass.
It is there, as stubborn as our

mortality, as our struggle for wholeness
that never ends

but returns always to its beginnings
altered by its experiencings

ready to begin again

THE CALL

Alone, late at night,
at last an hour in which to
write a poem.
But if you sit all day at
the typewriter with another song
you don't make empty the
bowl that holds new flowers,
waiting for the pebbles,
its words, to make a new bed.

But a man needs many things
often at cross-purposes,
but only because he desires.
Is the poem as desire any better?
Not poems but words
that heal as water heals,
moving freely, tugging,
slowly putting the truth
before our eyes.

Words and water do not desire.

HE ISN'T HERE TO SAY

You don't have to stop or start
    you just have to continue
It is like that forever
    and it is good but
One day you look up and see
    that it is nothing like what
    you thought
And even what you are
    thinking now
It is not that either
    you didn't know
    and you don't know
But for once it bothers you
    because the plan is
    in you
But however you try
    you can't enter the plan
It must have been different once
    but you can't get back there
And it seems you can't go
    forward from here

This no beginning
    is the beginning

RECURRING

What is life but unlearning.
When we come to the end
we slowly pull ourselves
back to the beginning

Hand over hand we go
back into returning
and our gains, which are
no more than our losses,
are left behind

And this returning
is not to a place in time
but to ourselves
outside of time
and all remembrance of self.

DARKNESS

The stillness of the night
when you are alone,
can anyone say it. The dark
breathing, the dark crackling
silence, the dark death of night.

And where am I in myself.
And what after all these years do I know
and what have I become.
To sit here like this is to be
reminded of one's life,
the strangeness of being who
I am, and all that I am not.
The day picks you up and takes you
but always it leaves you here,
here where you remember yourself
and see again the same desperate life.

We are not big enough for the dark
we do nor know enough for the light.
Something else must enter here before
death does, death that cracks
us open, dispersing all color and sound.

157

THE DEATH / LIFE THING

When death comes it will take
the completed thing, ending
where it began,

Death is a living act
digesting itself and meeting
itself in a heightened moment

that can happen whenever we
are fully and truly alive,
when experiential time ends

when what we call life
and what we call death
join in their wholeness

AGAIN

Emptied glass of wine
and no roses, sky
and no sun—
a lifetime passes—

look up, the clouds
part the sky
or does the sky
part the clouds—
no signs, no warnings—
all or nothing
again

remember yourself—only
that—until sky parting
clouds the sun moves
into you, the
southern wind blows
open the doors
and takes you there.

THE HOUR OF TESS

Three times I picked burdocks
from her tail:
once in the chicken house
where I carried her round
my neck, startling the chickens,
the second time in the midst
of her terrifying a chipmunk
that got away, and the third
time on the coverlet of the
guest room bed. And now she
sleeps on the other end of the
couch—while I write these lines—
one paw over her nose
that divides her eyes in half.

NONNY HOGROGIAN

Hogrogian means earth carrier
in the language of our ancestors,
and now Nonny takes up the tools
of her new trade, putting the
tools of art aside for the moment—
to actualize something new, that
is as old as our people, whose
beginnings precede Biblical time,
knowing, as she has always known,
that to work is to enter mystery
(the oldest mystery being earth
and its turning), by making new
forms out of combinations of old
materials. A garden, an idea as
old as Eden, from where the
beginning of knowledge moved out
into the coming, as yet unmade world.

THE TWO

I married an earth-carrier.
My father spaded his garden.
She often says she would have
liked him, understood his ways,
like the daughter who brings
her father things, smiling,
expecting nothing, already
receiving heart exchange.

He would have been at home
with her, forgetting even
the ocean breeze of his country
settling in the plain where
the storks made their homes
in the village trees.
But he died before she came
into my life, returning
to earth years ahead of my
earth-carrier's time.

THE POET ADDRESSES
HIS DOUBLE

Don't look for answers.
It is not like that.
And it is not about that.
Organization is death,
to hold is to lose,
to give away is to keep.
I know, you've heard it all
before. Let go then.
It's balance you need,
not control.
Submit! Say yes!
Don't try to work it out,
you'll only make another mess.
Enter your life, only that.
Thank God, and be yourself.

TESSIE'S

What if the cat sleeps all the evening
 between two people (on her own chair)
 while they go on reading, looking at
 catalogues, studying magazines,
 and discussing urgent & impending work

Because earlier she lay on the tabletop
 (next to the woman peering
 through her fur with an instrument
 for untangling knots) while
 the man held her front & back paws
 and took the bites in his fingers
 that she meant, warningly

And now she sleeps, deep in the
 emotional warmth of people
 who need her, not knowing why
 as she needs them, not needing
 to know why

Because somewhere it is known
 that sleeping or awake
 something for them
 is being transmuted by her
 for a purpose she and they
 do not need to understand.

AGAIN BEGINNING

The careful working of a woman's hands
    brooding over the shirt, folding,
    holding it up,
    turning and placing it on the pile
of already folded clothes

How often we sat like this
    in days passed, making a life
    and poetry—
its meaning belonging
    to an order of art—
    and ordered as art—
all because of fear that life
    did not mean enough
    or that its meaning was
not enough for us.

But now we know that the meaning does
    not come from us—
    but that we can enter into
    the meaning as it exists,
    and as we are.

Just ourselves, here, moving
    through a day of sorrows—
the sorrows of any life,
    lived and faced down
without excuse or apology
    and most importantly
without sentimentality.

And we come to the end of a day
  writing, folding clothes,
  with the cat, Tessie between us
  on the Oriental rug
  making her everyday toilet
in the midst of our everyday lives.

POSTSCRIPT

Are there endings or only new beginnings, time without end. After Morris, we continued our nomadic wanderings, driven in great part by our teaching, that has never left us, although many of our forays into encounters with Work groups were largely unproductive. More importantly, I wrote of our years in the Work in my book, ON A SPACESHIP WITH BEELZEBUB: BY A GRANDSON OF GURDJIEFF. This summing up was important for us, and helpful to others, who like us were not stuck in old footprints and could find their own individual paths forward, as we had ours. The Work, like all authentic teachings leads to a better way of life, and the living of that life, free of dogma and imitation and hierarchy.

There have been many books of poems since, and other writings, but no further poems about our love or marriage, being one and the same, and so deeply central to our life, that it didn't need examining, nor the exigences of art to mark its continuance. Love is like that, it has no end, and can only grow in greater truth and beauty.

CODA

To wake up suddenly
feeling gratitude for one's life
and everything in it,
which for me boils down to two things:
my wife and my work, that I will not
position as separate,
being two miracles that occurred to me—
bestowed upon me, that I do not feel I earned,
although at the start I claimed that I would die
if I did not write, as now I know that I would
have died long before now if I had hesitated,
and if Nonny had not come into my life and stayed.

I want gratitude now to take over my life,
to never leave me alone—
no vacations, no days off—
instead here with me always,
along with pencil and tablet,
and even when idle,
to know these two comprise one life,
conjoined and blended, stirred into an elixir
I cannot live without,
for which I must always be grateful,
and never forget.

ABOUT DAVID KHERDIAN

David Kherdian is the author of more than eighty publications whose many awards include the Newberry Honor Award for THE ROAD FROM HOME. As a team, Nonny Hogrogian and David Kherdian have produced countless children's books as well as three journals as editor and art director: *Ararat, Stopinder: A Gurdjieff Journal for Our Time*, and *Forkroads: An Ethnic American Journal.*

ABOUT NONNY HOGROGIAN

Nonny Hogrogian is the illustrator and/or author of 75 books, having twice been awarded the Caldecott medal, as well as a Caldecott Honor Book. With her husband David Kherdian they launched the first and only press to present the work of the mystic, G. I. Gurdjieff, the first master, to bring Eastern spirituality to the West, and whose sacred dances are now performed around the world.

Cascade Press

Made in the USA
Middletown, DE
13 September 2024

60400621R00097